A Quieter Path of Peace

Words by Janet Kathleen Ettele
Photography by J. Gregory Raymond

Graphic design by Pattie Copenhaver

Library of Congress Cataloging-in-Publication Data is available upon request.
ISBN 9780578619941

Peace to all who enter

Each moment of thought
is like brush strokes on a canvas.
With awareness, know what you are creating.

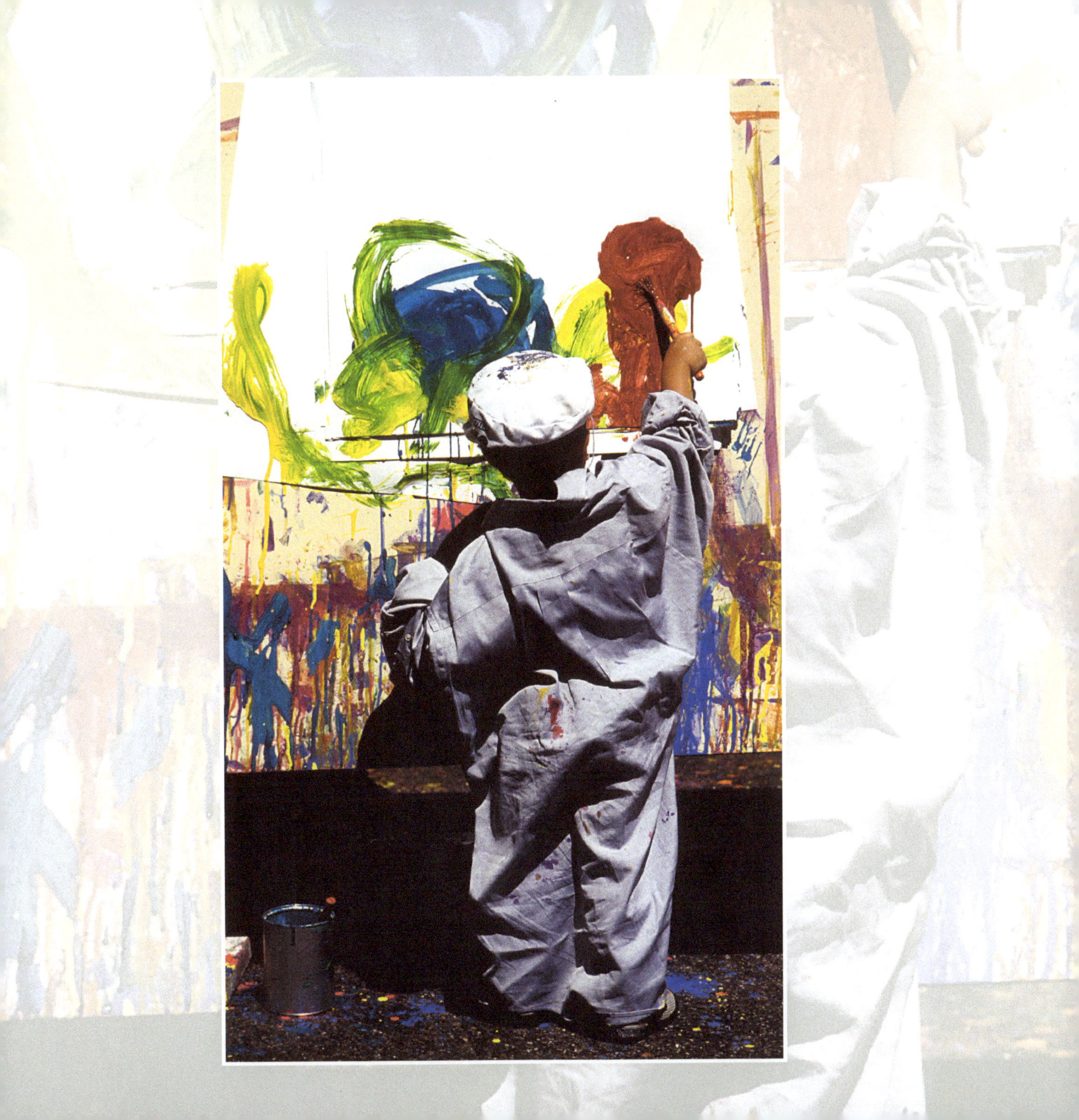

When we strengthen our thoughts,
we strengthen their manifestation
in our outer experience.

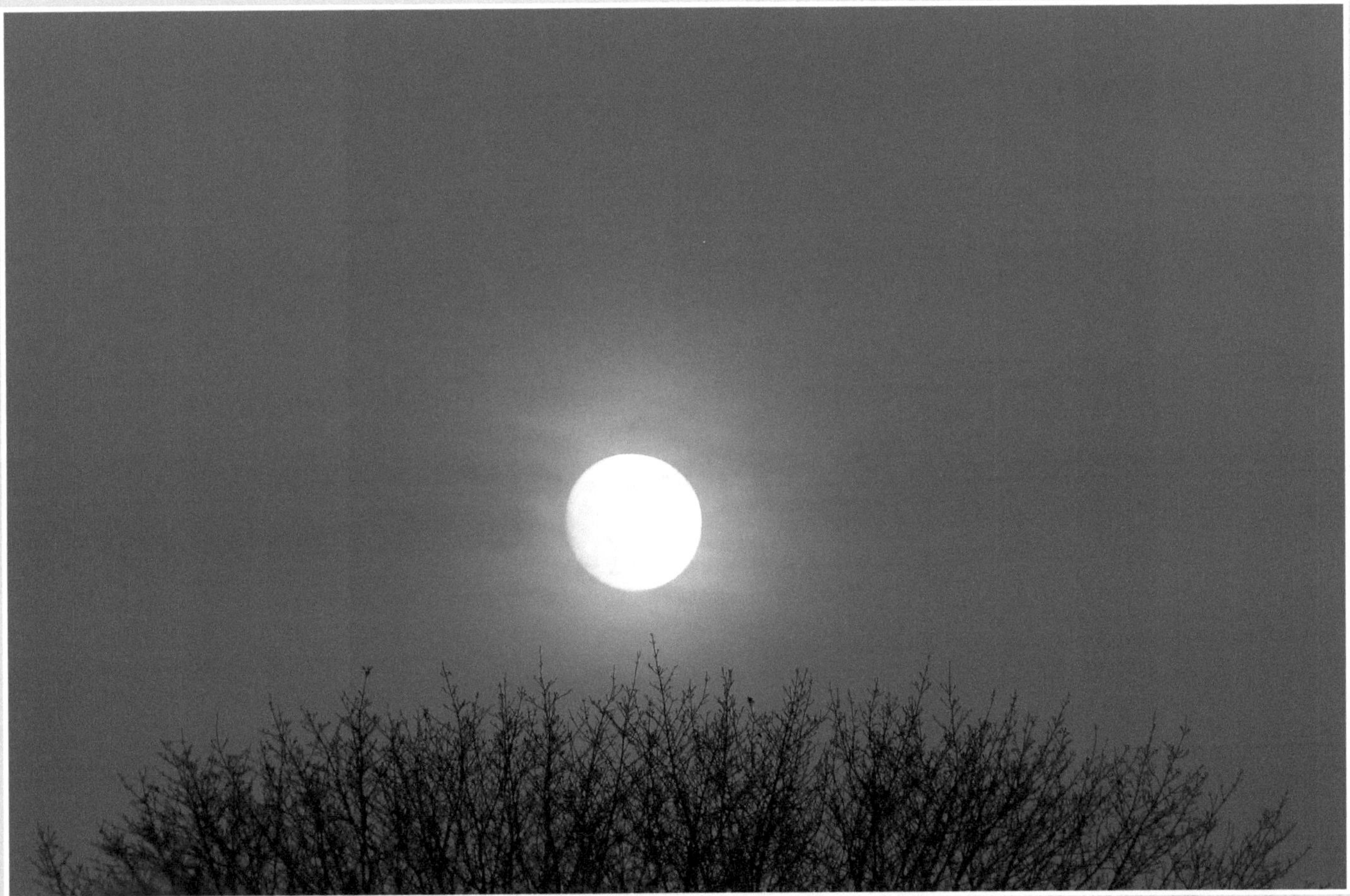

Think of karma like a game of pool,
your life as the cue ball and your thoughts
as the cue. Aim skillfully.

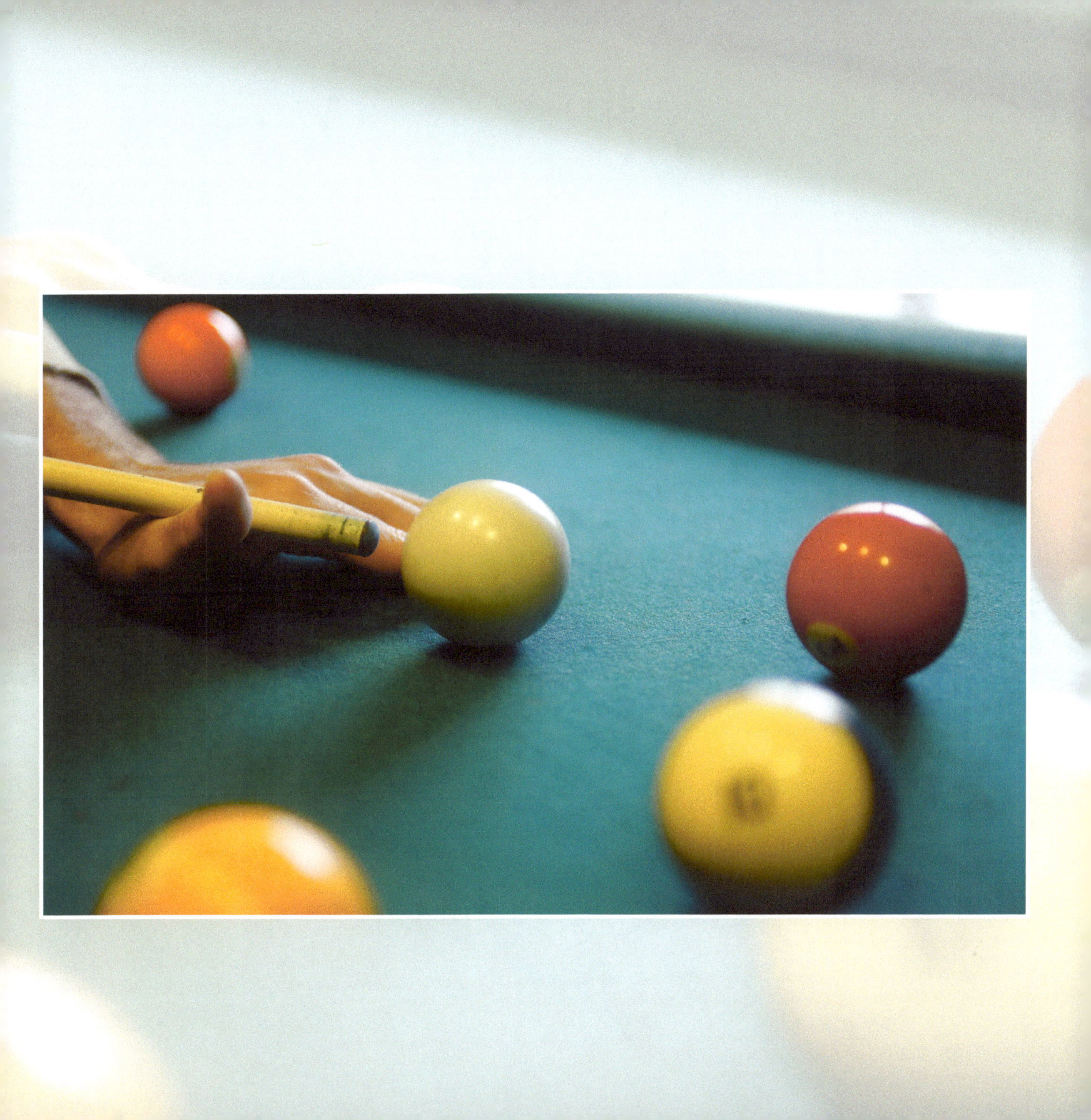

If the mind is clear the path will be clear.
If the mind is angry the path will be angry.
A mind of peace is the path to peace.

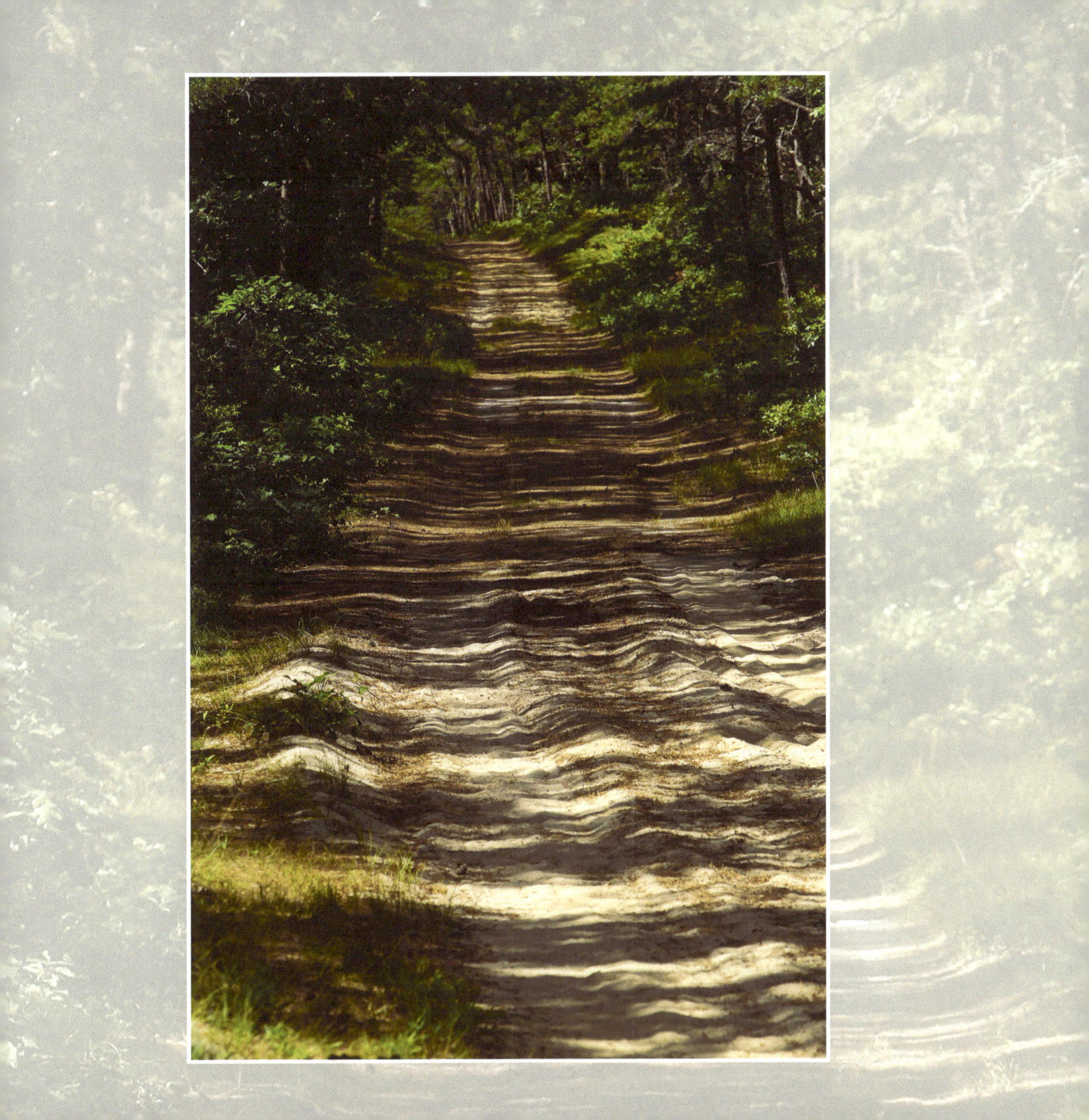

Wisdom is like an infinite cosmic reservoir.
With a thirst for understanding a seeker
will find its source.

Even if it is just a whisper, if you quiet your mind you will hear the gentle voice of love, and from there it grows.

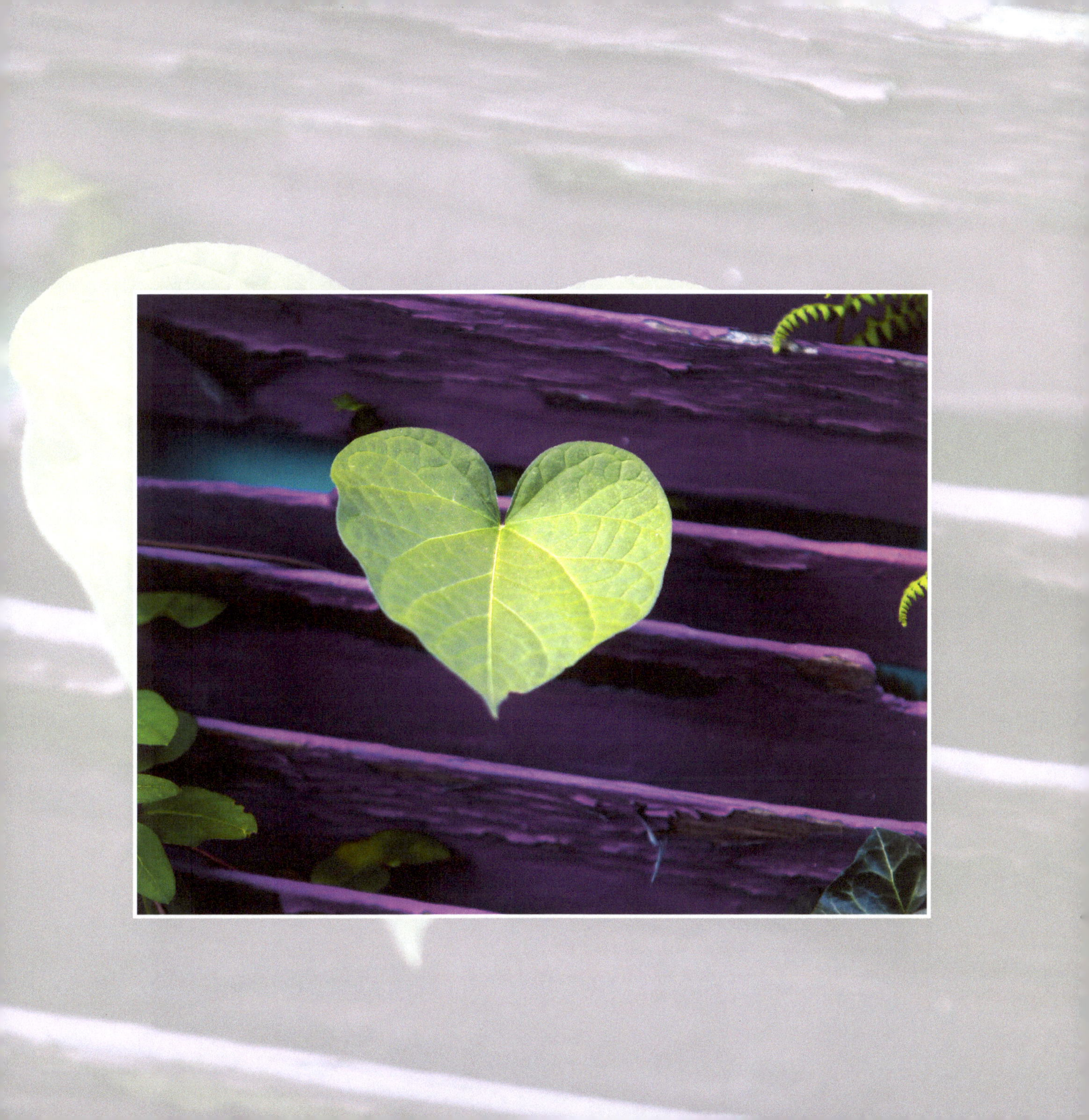

You can't open a rose before its time.
Be patient and remember that we all need light to grow and thrive.

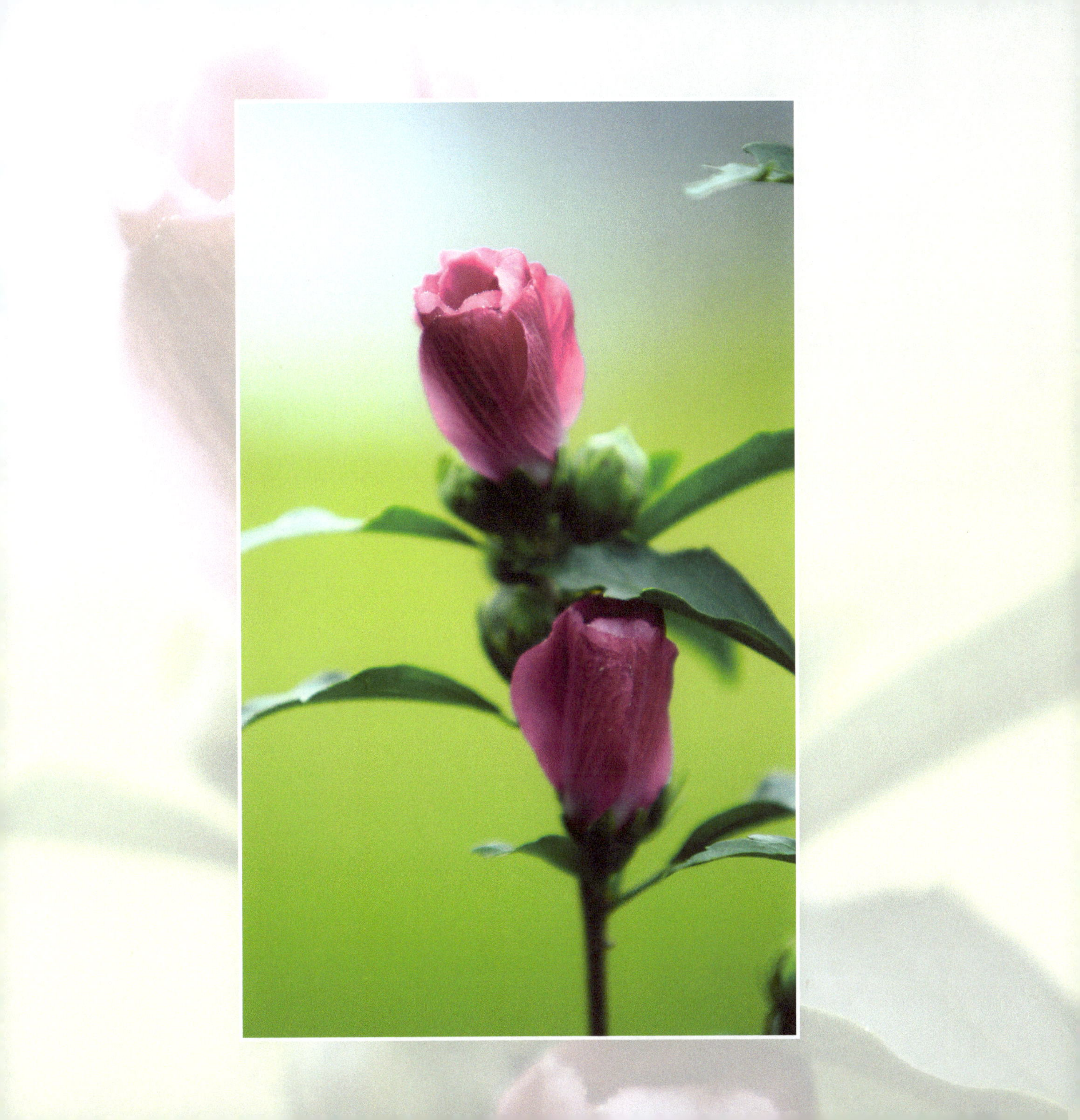

The practice of patience will not fail to deliver the more powerful and controlled energy to eliminate anger.

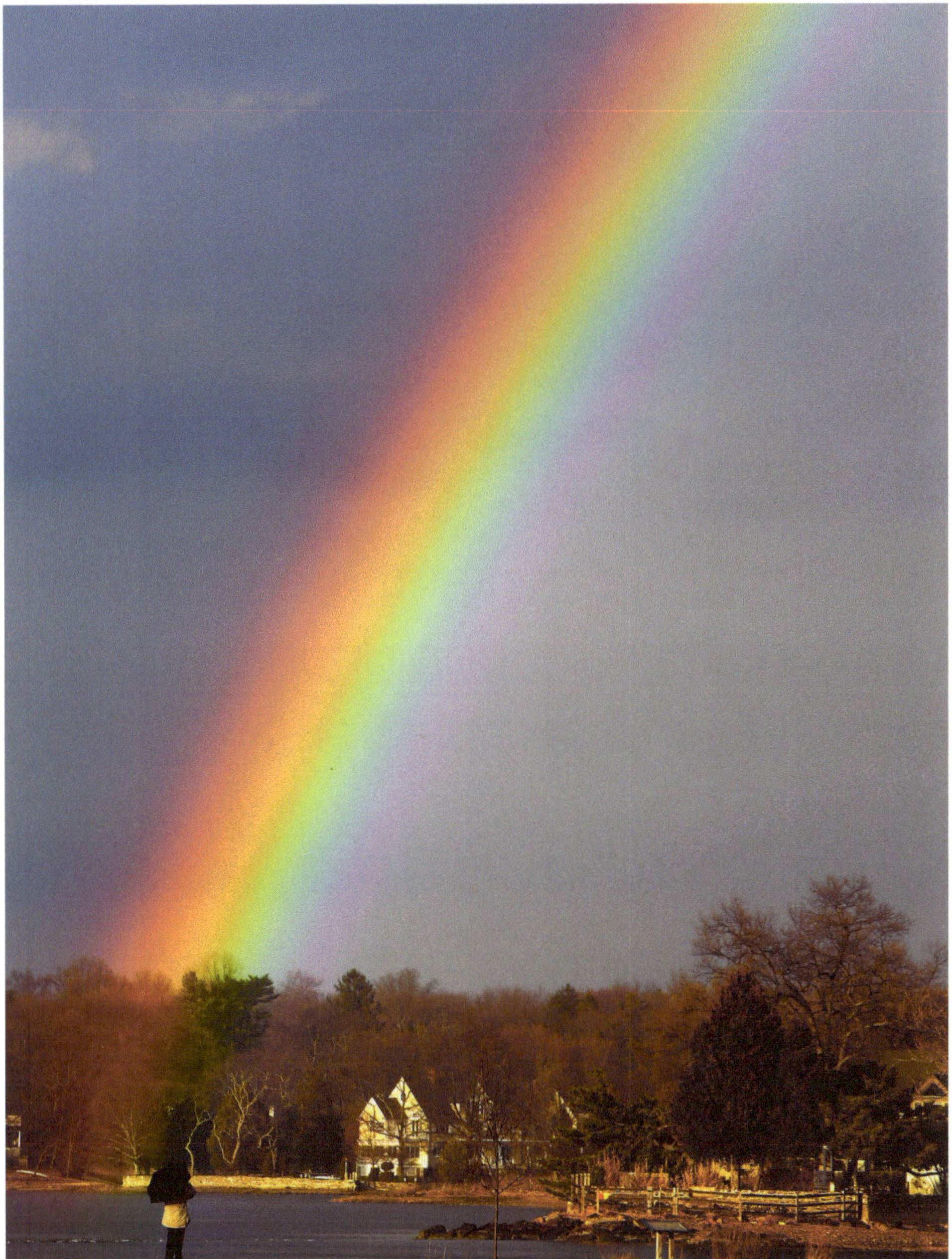

Without interdependence there could be no life. If we look deeply, the opportunities to express gratitude and compassion are endless.

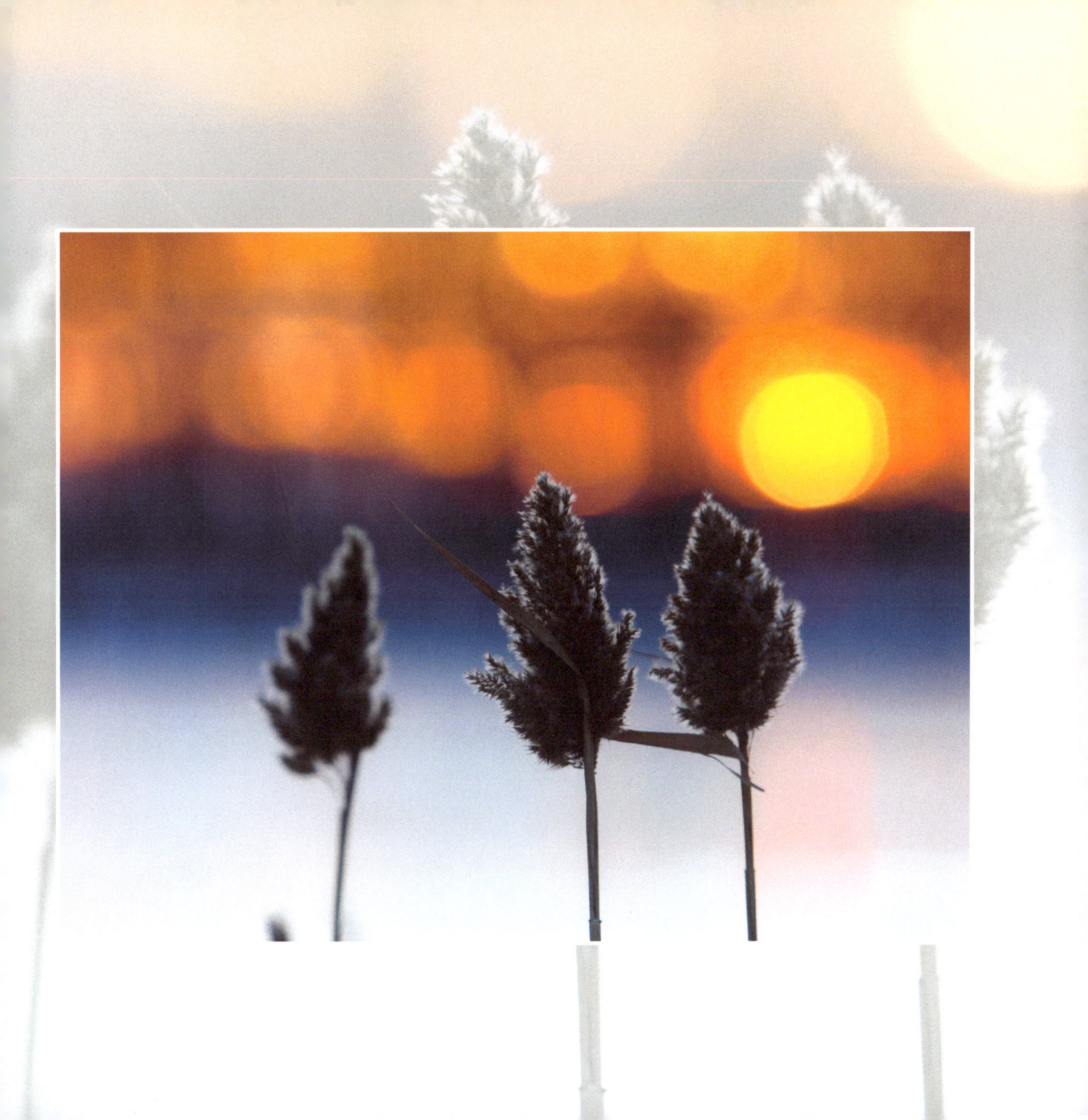

Attraction brings bias. Aversion brings dislike.
Strive to reduce both.

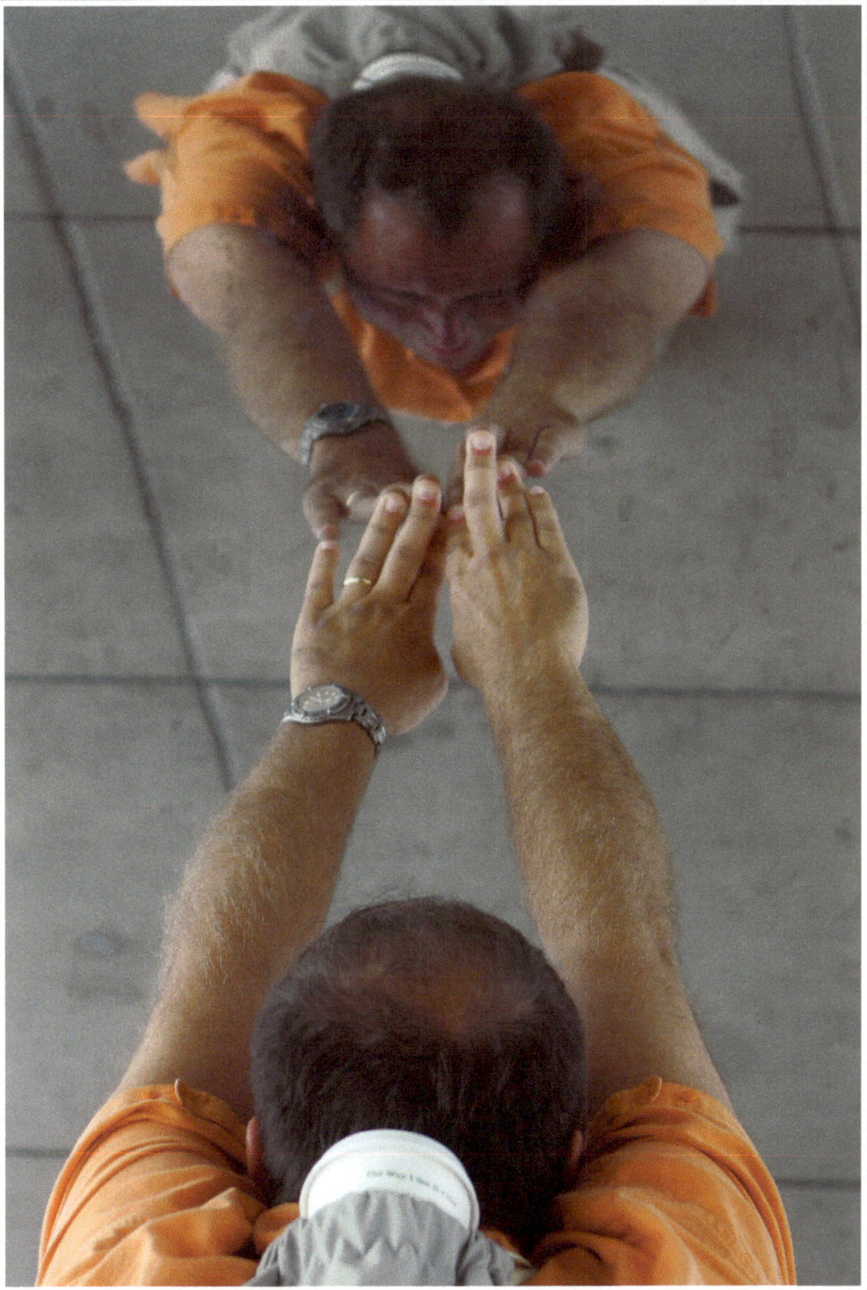

Ignorance is like mental blindness that cannot see that everyone and everything is interdependent.

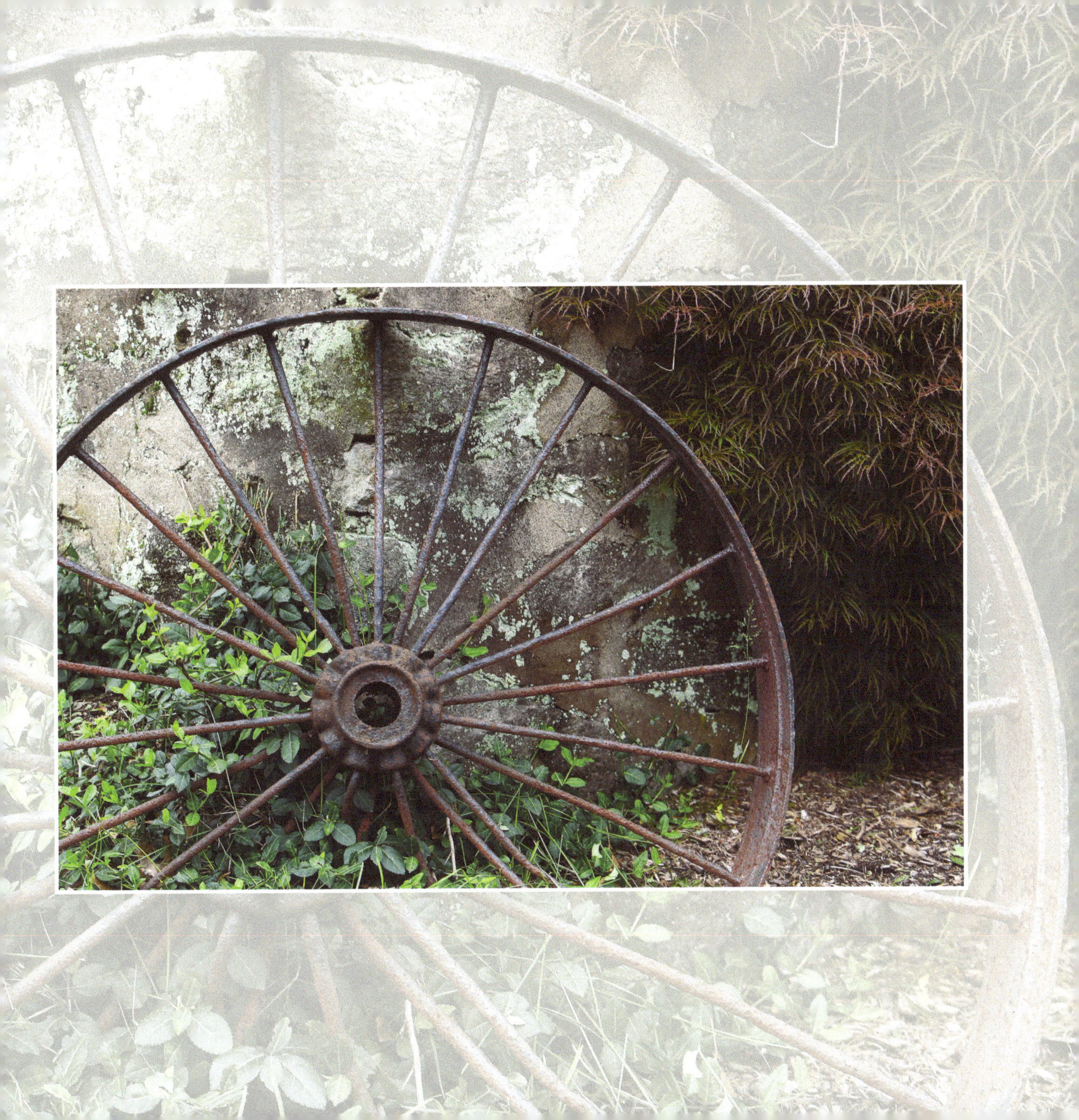

The lasting method to heal a broken heart is to offer love and compassion to others.

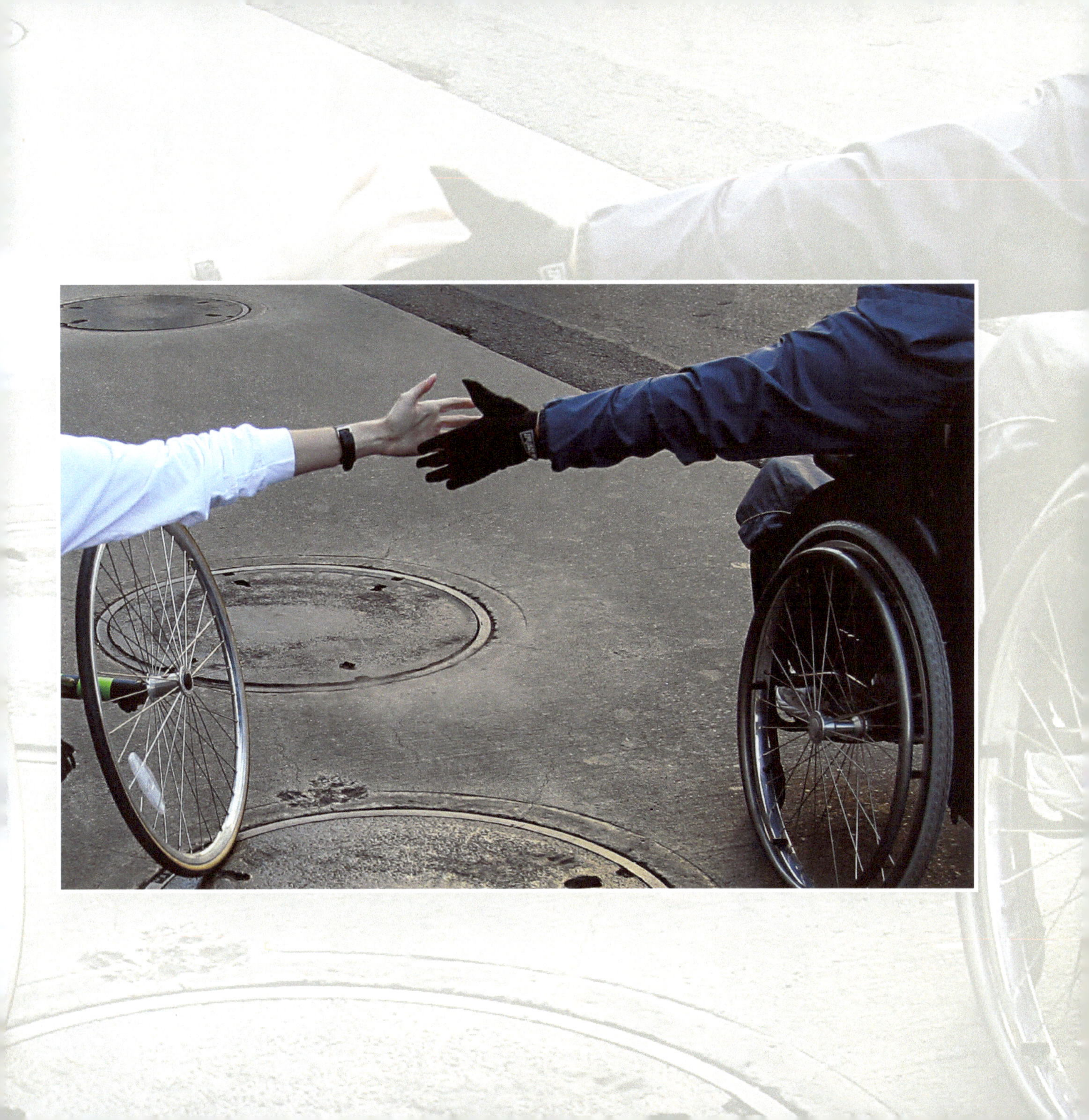

You are the light that plays
between the song and the dance.

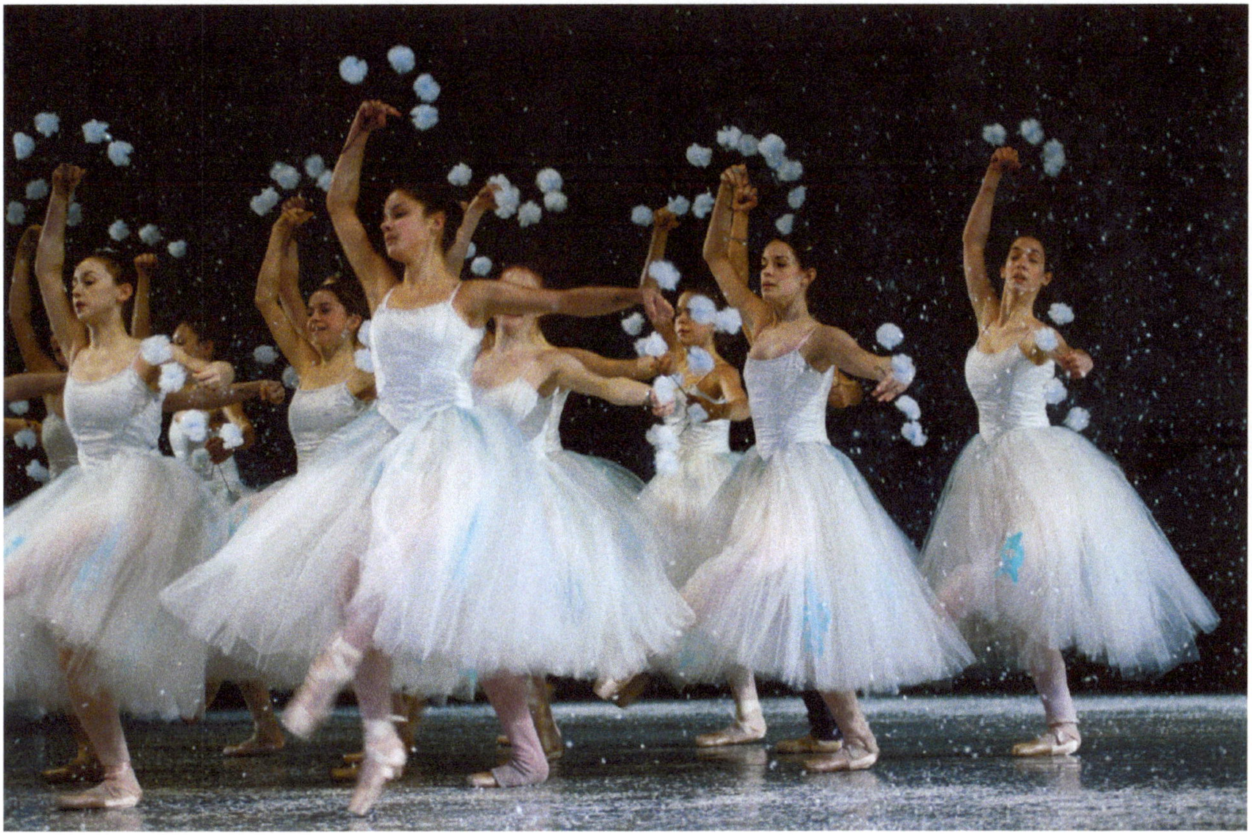

If we train our minds to be aware of the
symbiotic nature of all that exists,
then causing no harm we would offer only
love and compassion to all.

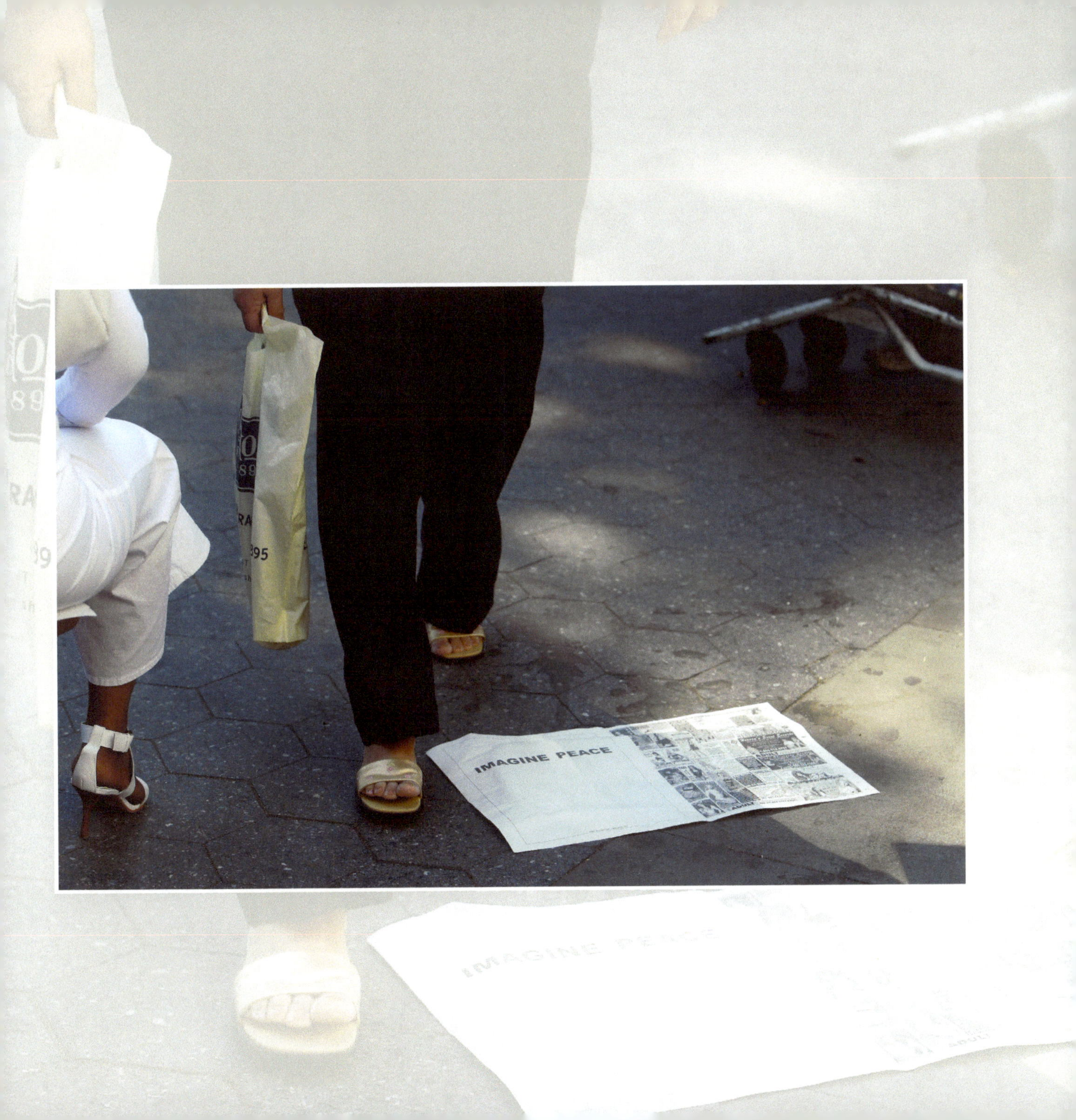
IMAGINE PEACE

Releasing the grip of attachment is where freedom exists to truly enjoy what is, what has been, and what is yet to be.

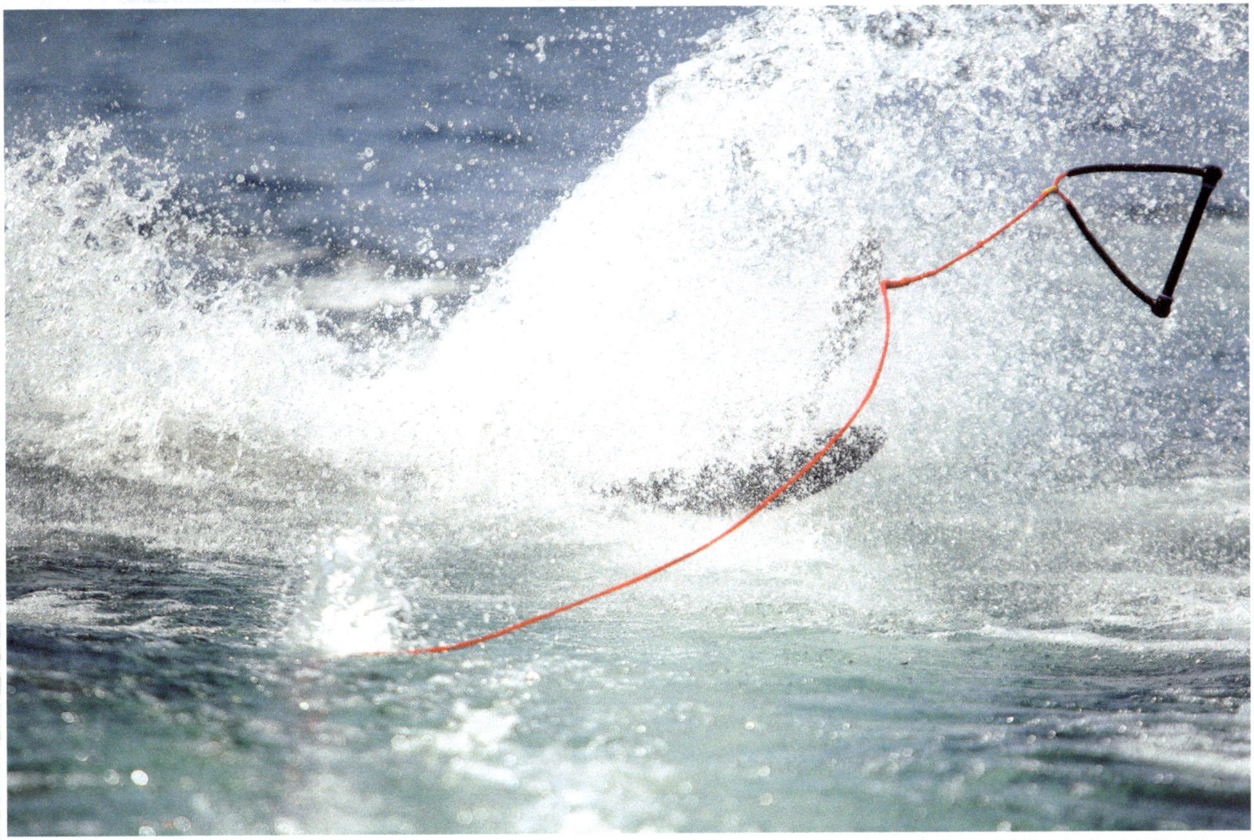

Comprehend there is no real separation between one and another and you will uncover the power to convert disharmony into peace.

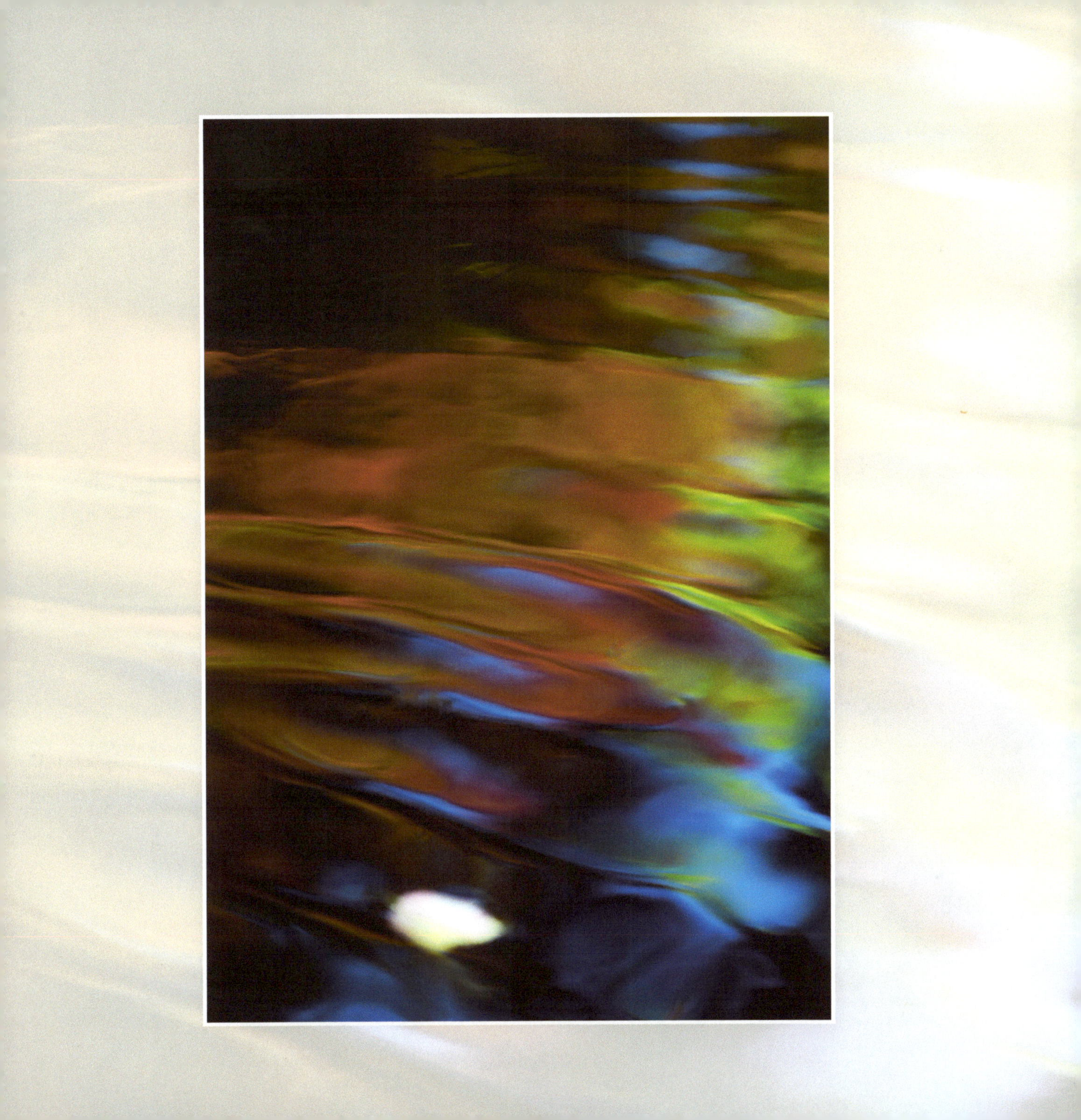

Because no one and no thing exists by itself there can be no true peace until all are free from suffering.

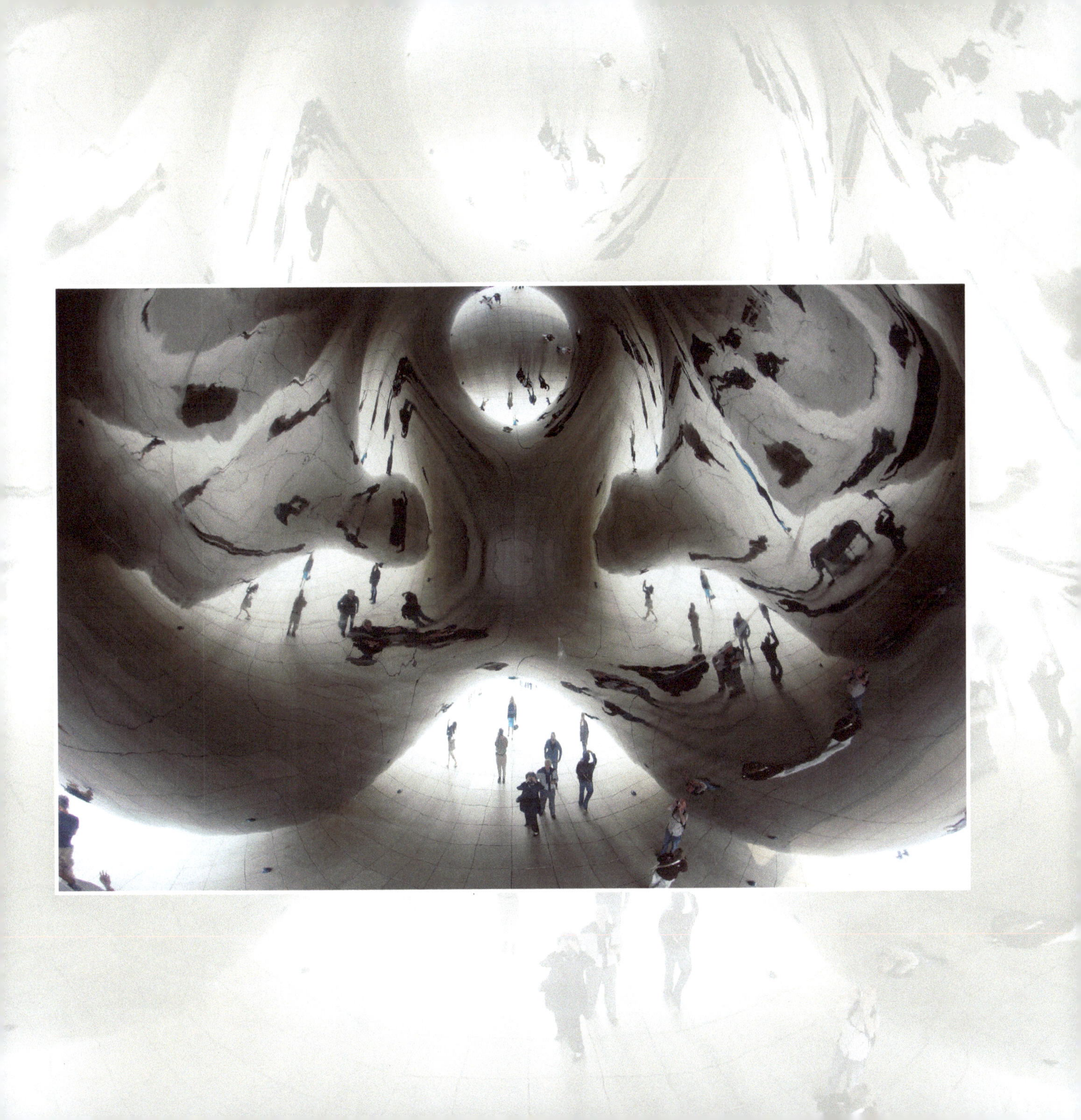

Your nature is creative by the very fact that you are alive and capable of thought. Your life is your poetry, your song, your art, and your masterpiece.

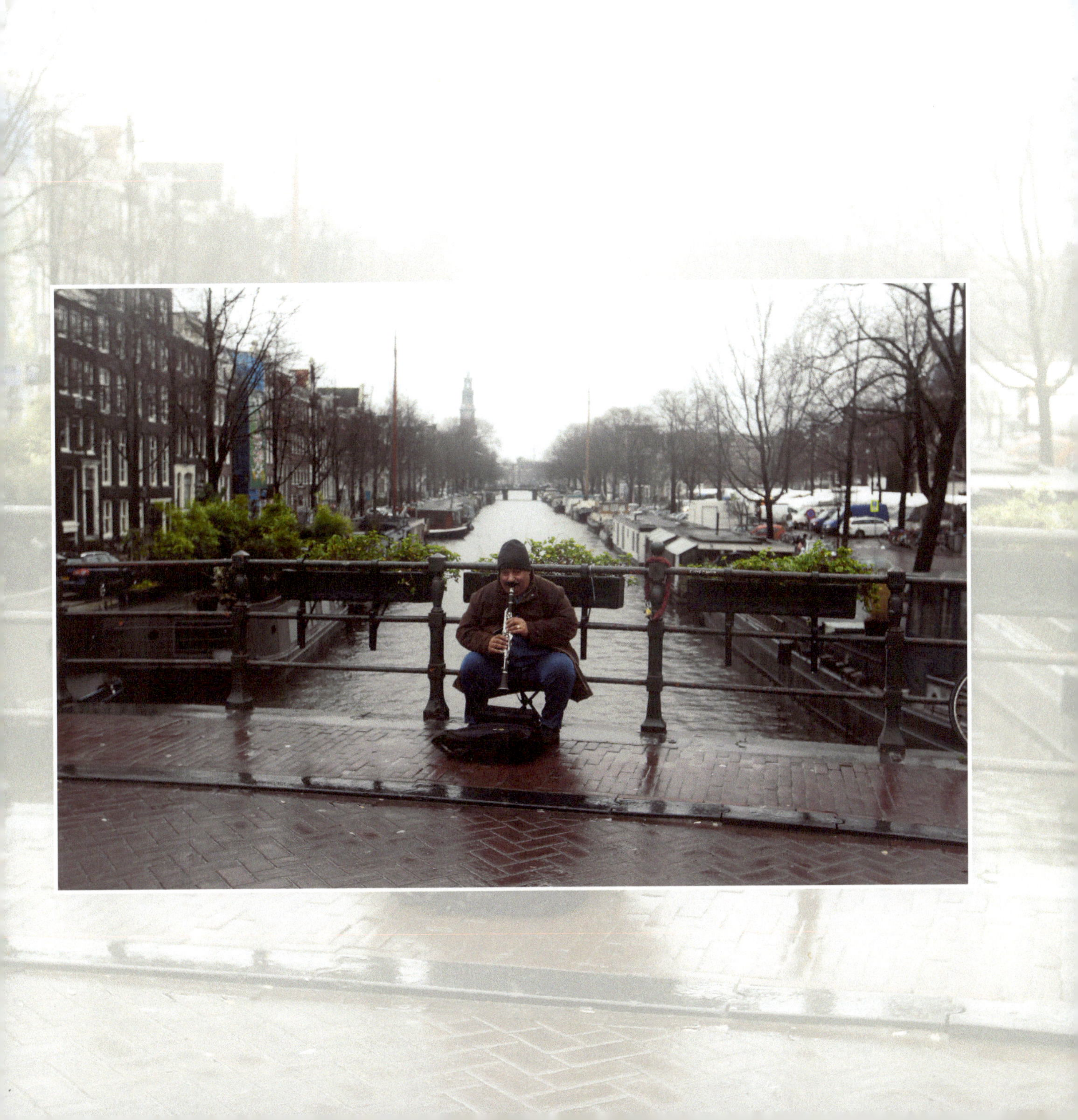

Regardless of faith or tradition, true peace is not naïve optimism but an achievable reality that begins with a wise and compassionate mind.

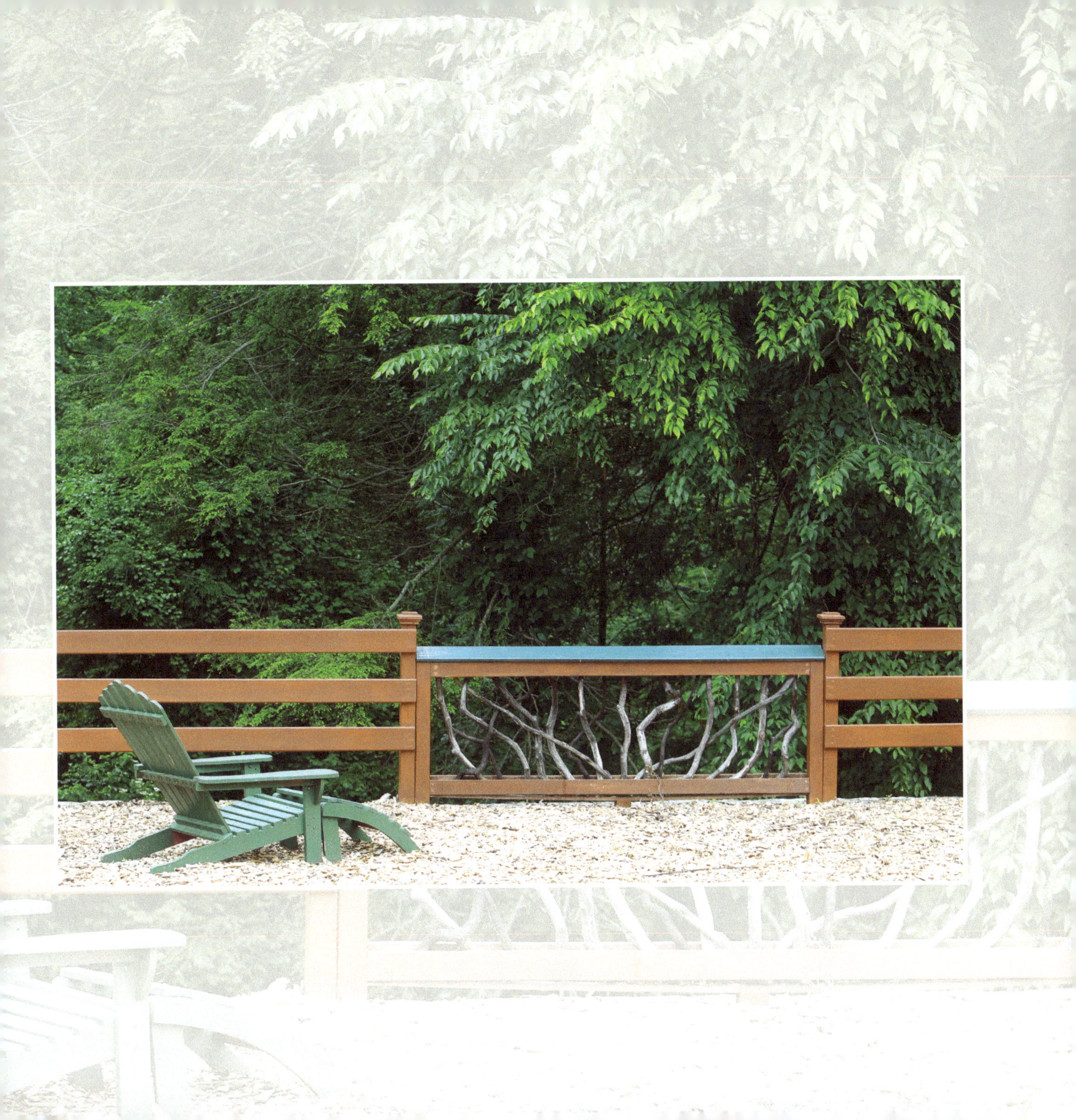

Maybe it simply is like gardening, meeting the conditions each day presents—some days are for tilling, others to plant, weed, harvest, or rest.

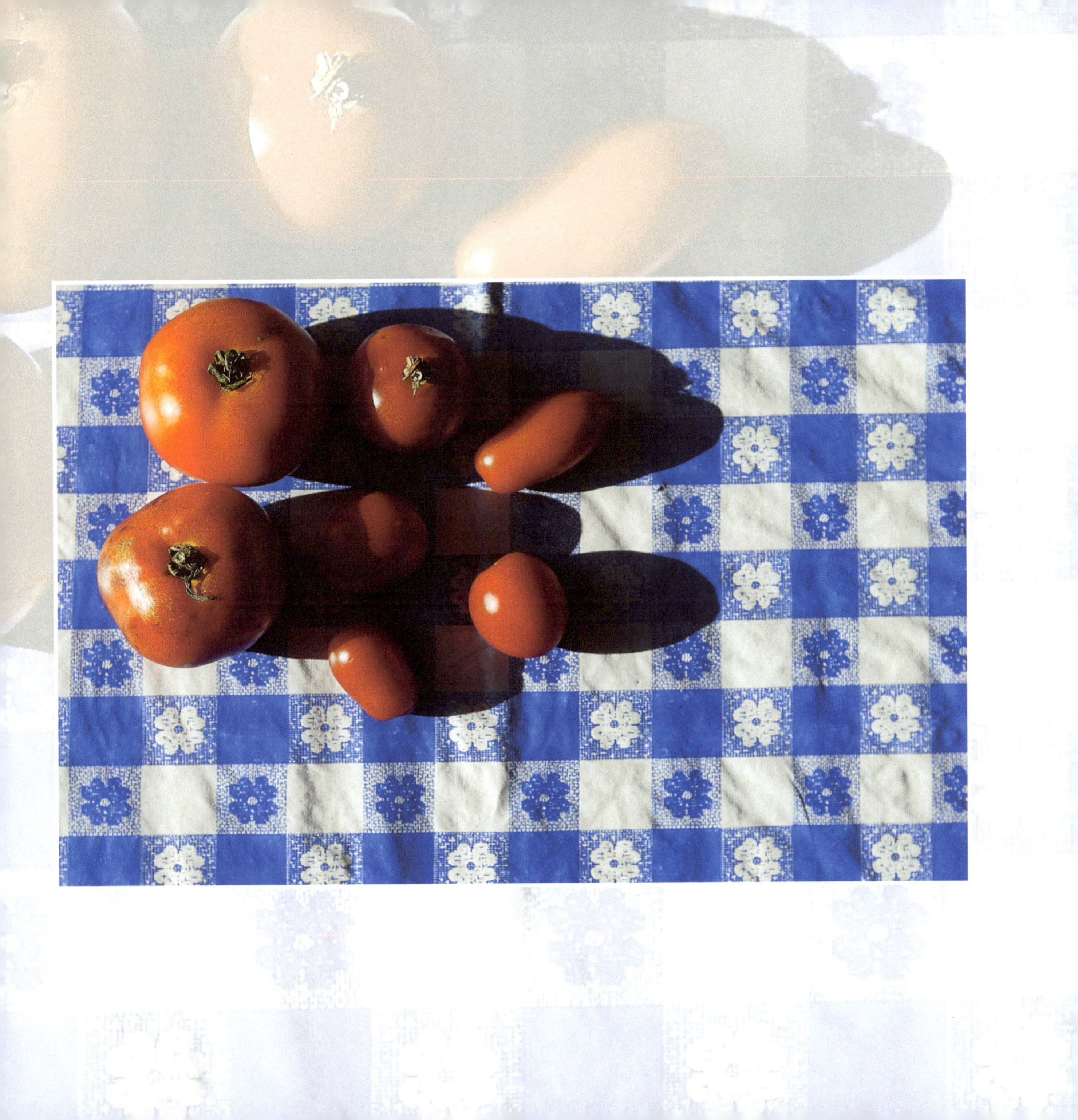

This life will come to its end but the mind continues as it's been conditioned. Cultivate loving kindness for all and peace will follow.

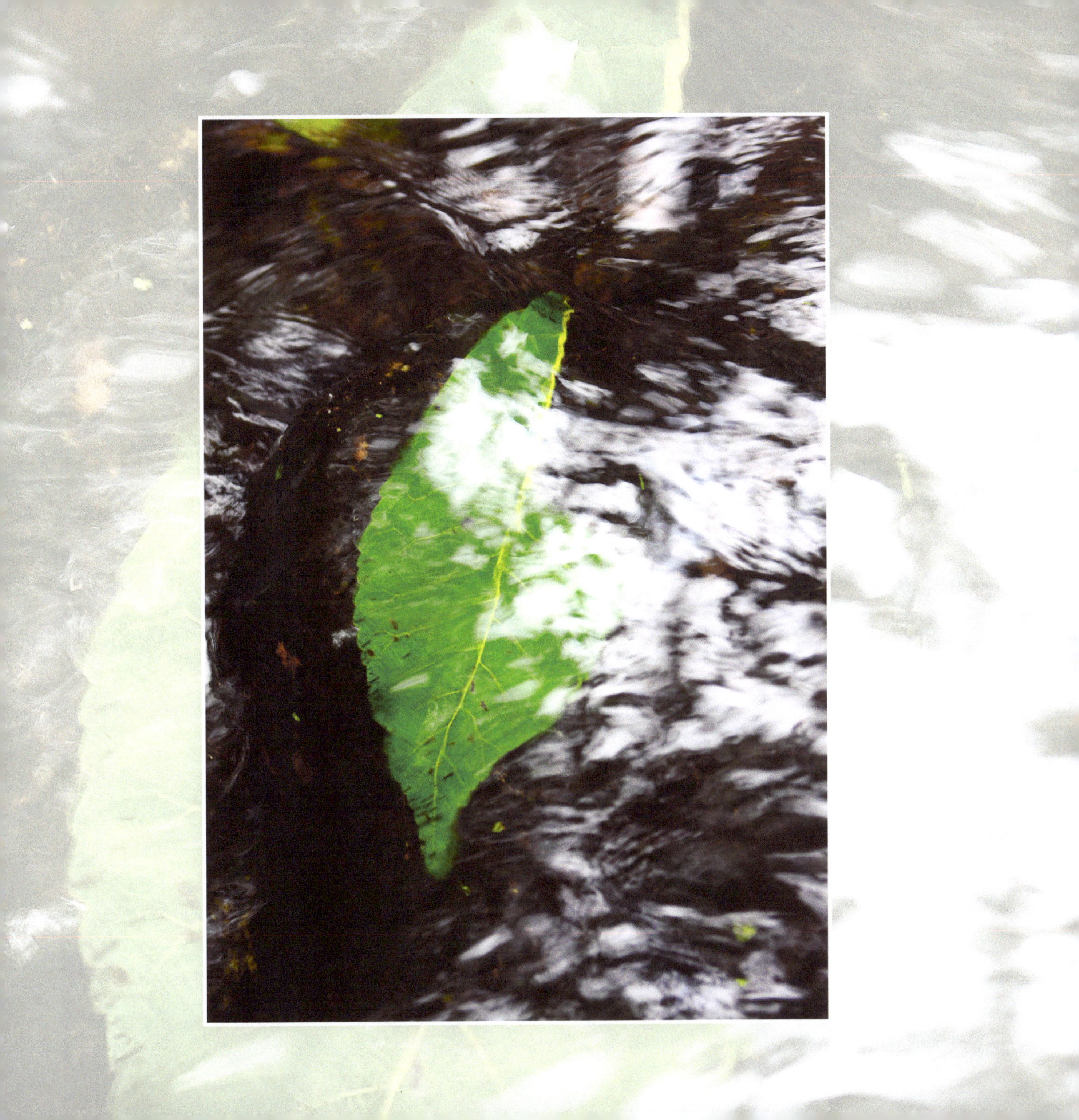

A moment of awareness can unveil truth
that hides behind delusion.
Engage it and see how things change.

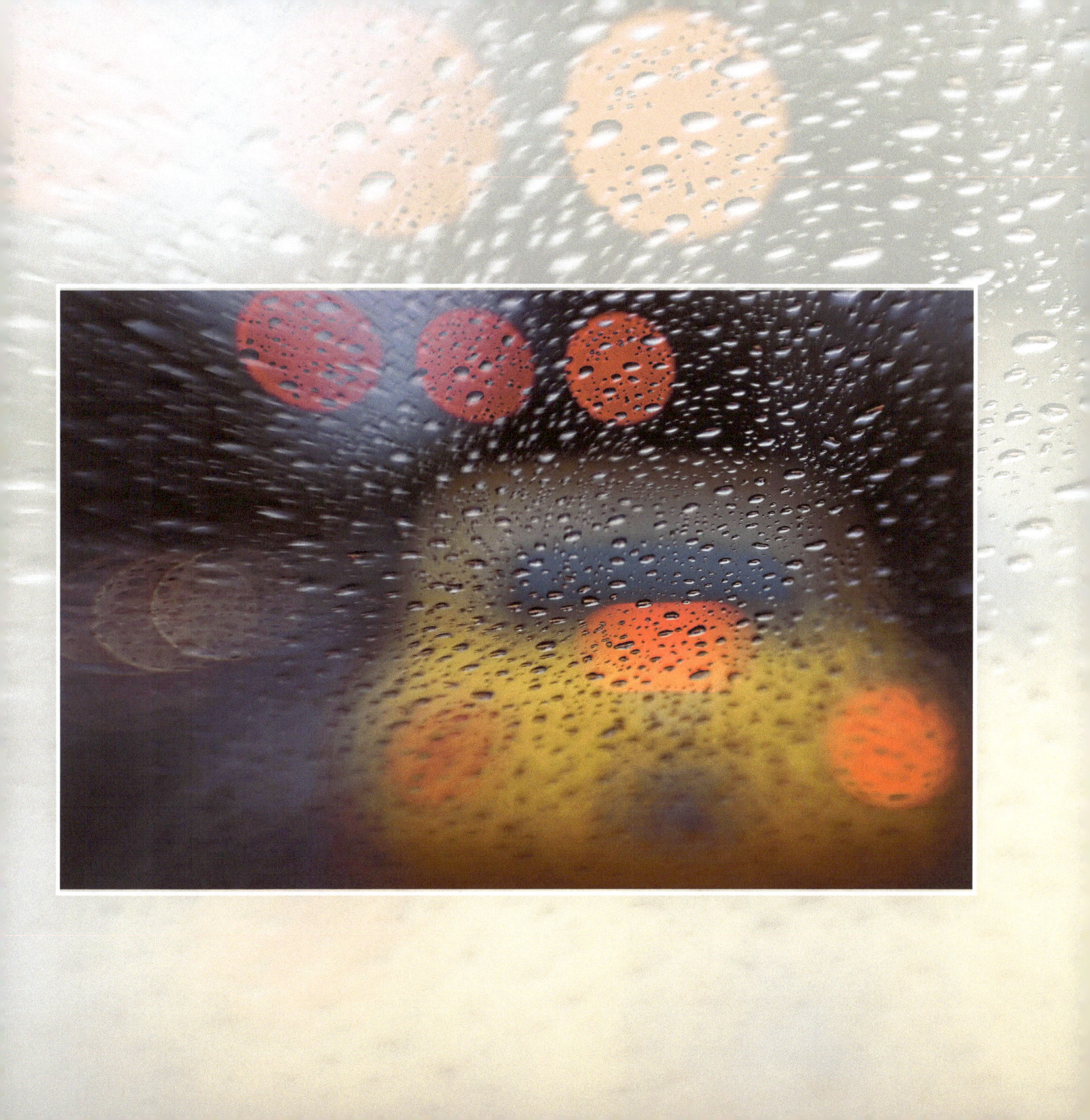

Hold all of life gently and lovingly
like a butterfly in a hand and there
will be no pain from clinging and attachment.

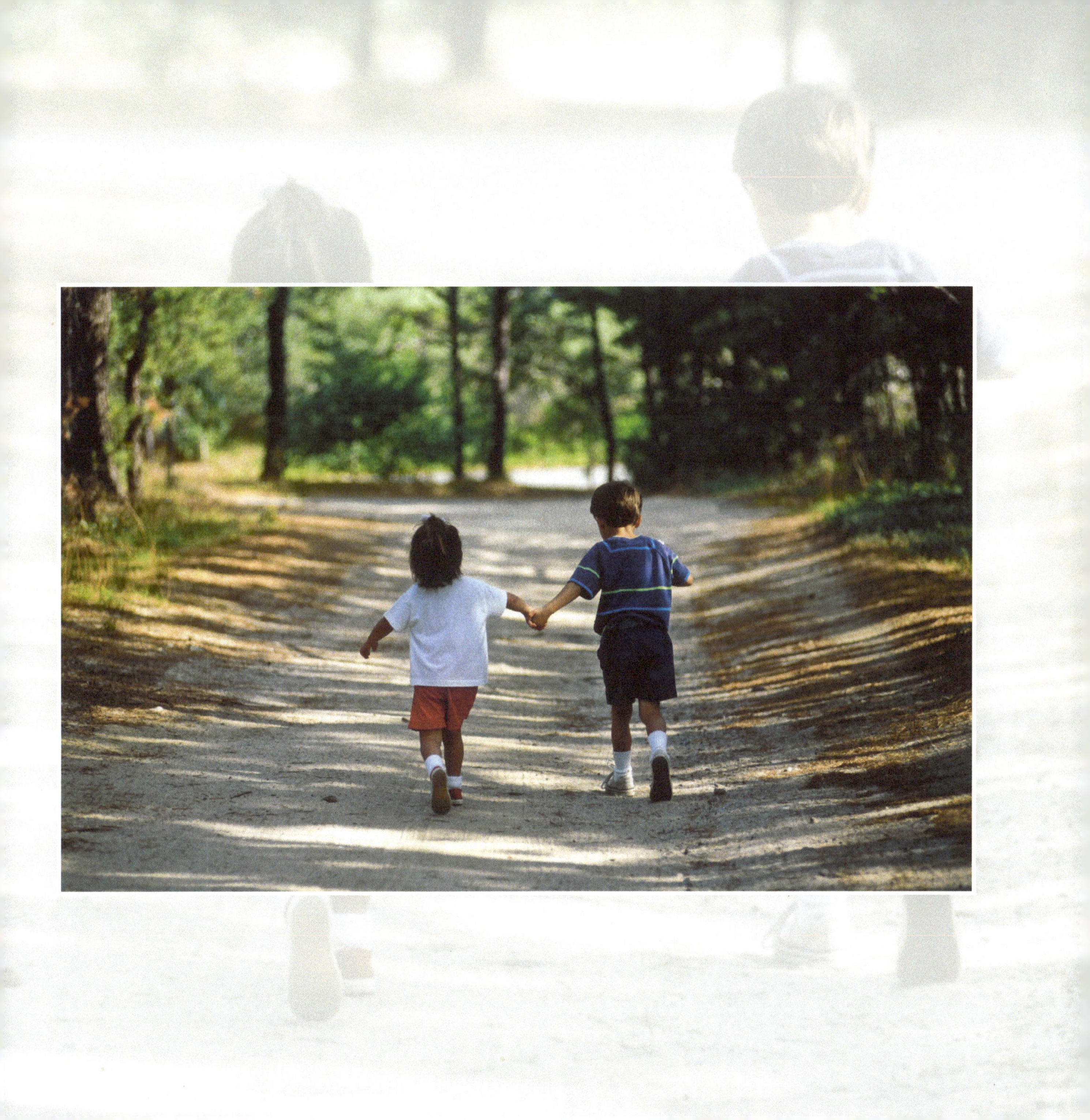

Cultivate wisdom to meet death for what it is,
like slipping into another day carrying the
accumulations of the day before.

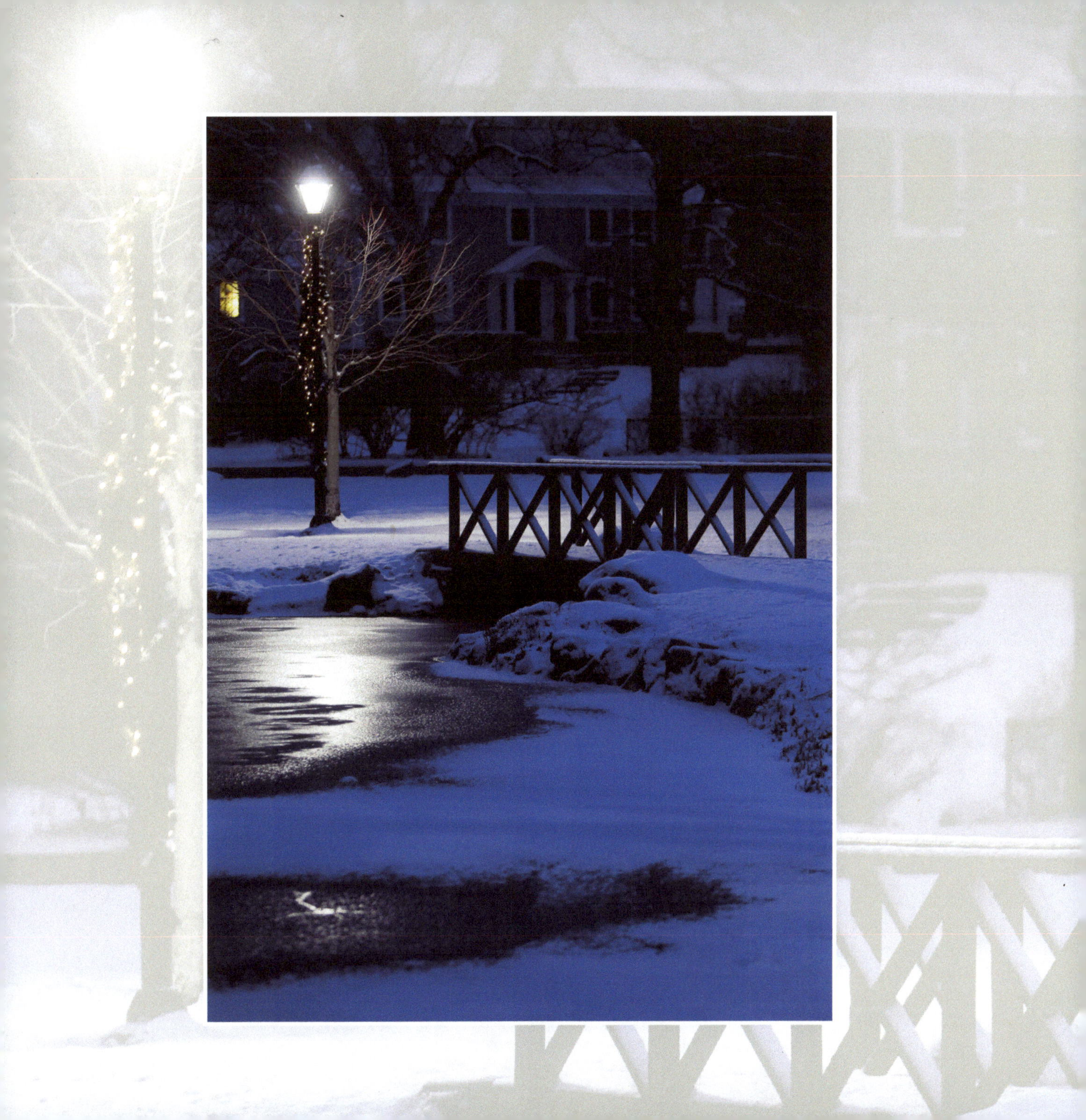

Beyond the limit of words,
wisdom's voice is silence.

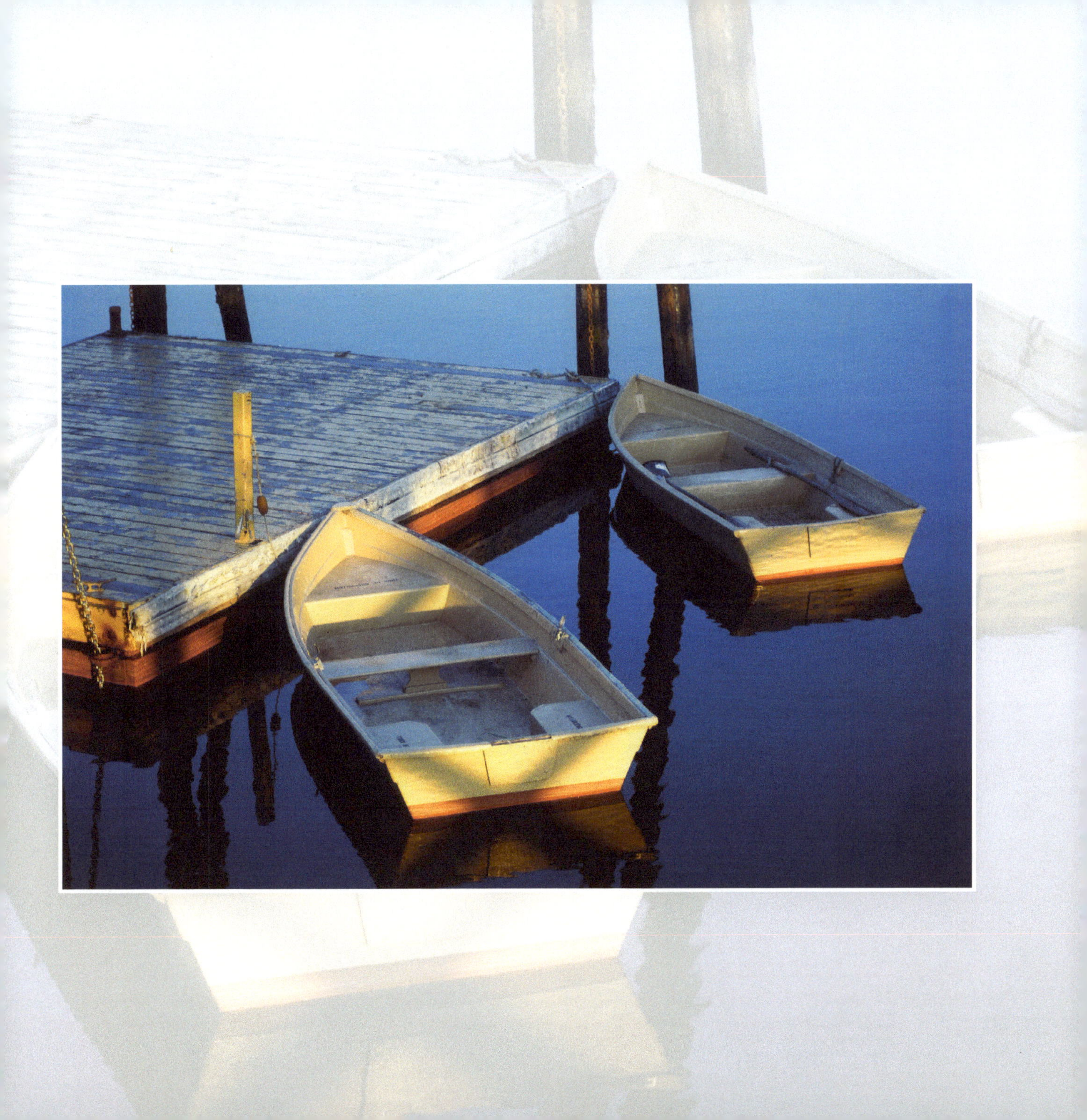

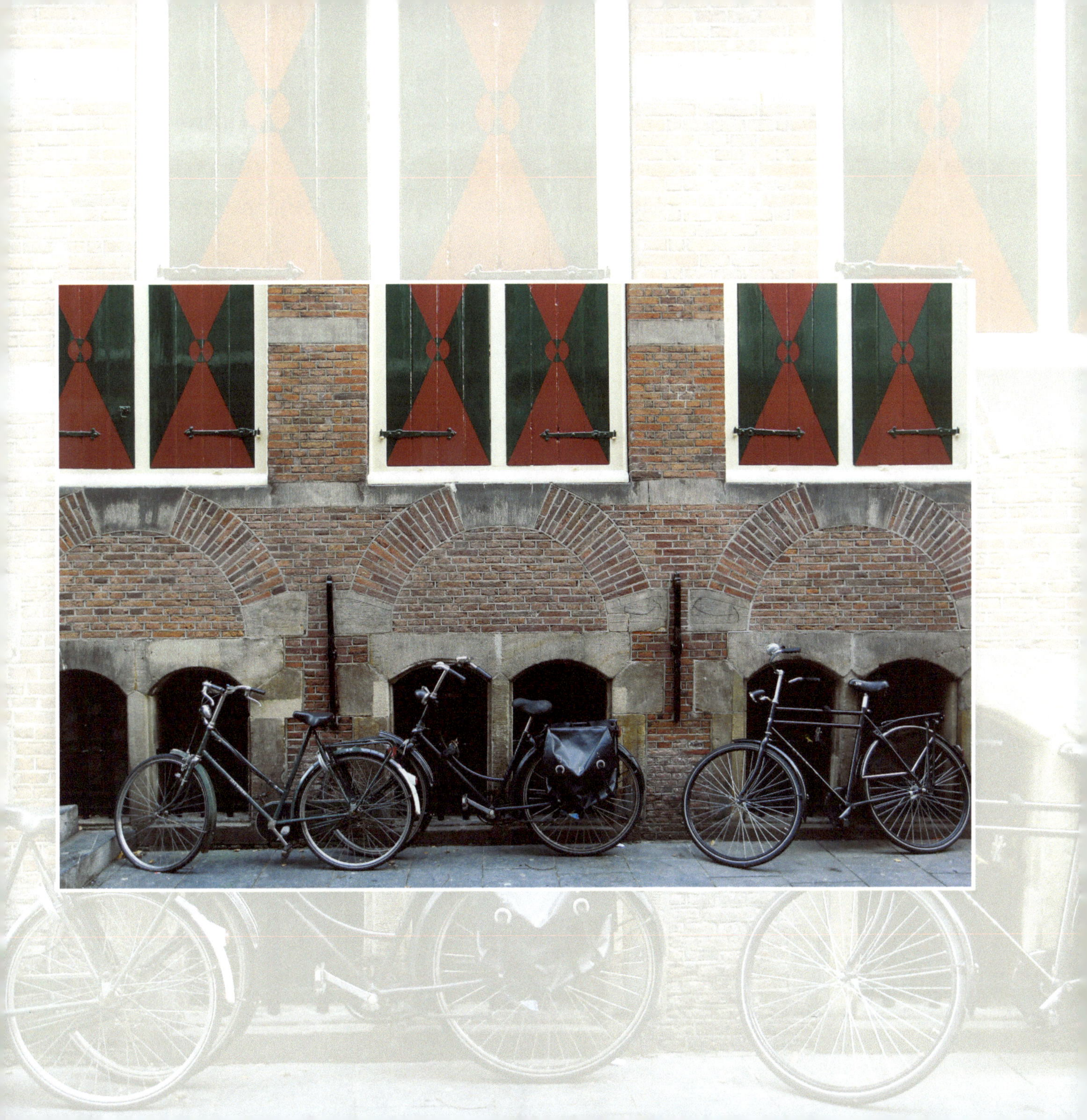

Janet Kathleen Ettele is an author, a life coach specializing in mindfulness based coaching, and musician who draws on her background as a student of Buddhist dharma to bring its teachings into contemporary practice through her writing, coaching and her music.
http://janetettele.com

J. Gregory Raymond is a self-taught award winning photojournalist who specializes in editorial, sports, corporate, special events and portrait photography. A 2010-2011 recipient of "Who's Who in North American Photography," Greg takes over 30 years of experience into each assignment. His images have appeared in major magazines, newspapers and Fortune 500 companies.
http://jgregoryraymond.com

ISBN 9780578619941

Words: Janet Kathleen Ettele
Photography: J. Gregory Raymond
Graphic design: Pattie Copenhaver